£1·00

INTRODUCTION

Eating for health is in vogue. People today are focusing on fitness, and a good way to achieve and maintain that fitness is through a healthy diet. This new food awareness is affecting almost everyone, as we all count calories and cholesterol while we keep up with today's full-throttle life-style.

There are no secrets to losing weight and then keeping it off. You don't need to follow a starvation diet, nor do you have to try all sorts of confusing, esoteric fad diets. The truth is simple: if you want to weigh less, you must consume fewer calories than your body needs to maintain itself. If you follow such a regime, your body will eventually begin to use up the matter it has stored for a rainy day, and the pounds will begin to disappear. Once you reach your ideal weight, you will want to stay at that point; this means eating on a regular basis just about the exact number of calories your body needs to maintain its weight, given your level of activity. Of course, if you cut back on the number of calories you are consuming every day, you must be careful to choose foods that give you maximum return on your calorie investment—foods that are high in vitamins, minerals, and protein and that give you a feeling that you've eaten. Therein lies the rub! Just as you want to be a good shopper and spend your money wisely, so you will want to spend your daily calorie allotment wisely, and go to bed at night feeling that you've eaten well but not to excess.

Dieting is a very personal thing. What works for your neighbor may not work for you. If you like low-calorie foods to begin with, then weight gain has probably not been a problem for you anyway, but if you relish those creamy sauces and sweet desserts, then finding satisfactory diet foods can be a problem. Make dieting an adventure instead. Think of it as a chance to try new foods and to experiment with different ways of preparing old favorites. Use more fresh herbs and spices to heighten the natural flavors in foods. Perk up dishes with a dash of lemon juice instead of pouring on a fattening sauce. At the end of your diet, you may find that your food preferences have changed, so that maintaining your ideal weight becomes easier and more fun.

The recipes in this book are all low in calories. They range from soups to desserts, and vary in calorie count accordingly. All are based on the freshest of ingredients, presented imaginatively and simply—yet they are reduced in fat, sugar, and salt.

Butter and other fats are not only high in calories but also in cholesterol. As a general rule, I reduce all butter in recipes by at least half and cook with a little water or wine for liquid. I also often steam foods to release their vital juices while retaining more vitamins and flavors. Instead of thickening sauces with eggs, cream, or starches, I often use a purée of vegetables. Stocks and broths may be reduced until thickening by boiling down and evaporating the water to concentrate the flavors. When I do use a thickener, I use cornflour or arrowroot to yield a lighter, clearer sauce at one-fourth the impact of flour (cornflour and arrowroot have twice the thickening power and half the calories of plain flour). Skim milk powder is also a quick and clever way to add protein and body to a white sauce without racking up a lot of additional calories.

Look to your markets for new products that can be used instead of the old standbys. Kefir cheese is now selling in many supermarkets as well as natural food stores; it is a creamy, low-calorie substance that will add flavor and body to foods. Neufchatel cheese, available on supermarket shelves right near the cream cheese, is a lower calorie spread that easily doubles for high-fat cream cheese. Substitute soured single cream for soured cream, and use canned evaporated skim milk instead of cream or regular evaporated milk. Buttermilk, low-fat curd cheese, ricotta, and plain yogurt are relatively low in calories, and can be splendid bases for creamy dips and dressings in place of high-calorie oils and butterfats.

Sugar and salt have been implicated in many diet-related health problems, so these recipes tend to be low in those substances. Sugar is high in calories with little nutritional benefit, while salt increases one's blood pressure and helps to retain fluids in the body. Although salt is a necessary dietary element, most people consume far too much of it. Packaged foods especially are high in sugar and salt, and you'll have an easier time dieting if you avoid such prepared foods. Instead, rely on fresh ingredients themselves, or purchase foods that specifically state they are lower in salt or are sugarfree.

The cooking and preparation times for the recipes in this book are short, because practically no one has the time to spend long hours preparing meals. The techniques are also very simple, and with the step-by-step photos right alongside, you should have great success making these dishes. The full-page photos on the facing pages will show you how the finished dish looks, and will give you ideas on garnishing your meals so they are as appealing to the eye as they are to the palate.

Good food can be truly filling without fattening. Experiment with these low-calorie dishes, and experience the fun of eating fresh foods while you lose weight.

UNDERSTANDING THE ANALYSES

For each recipe in this book, you'll note that we have provided data on the quantities of protein, fat, sodium, carbohydrates, and potassium, as well as the number of calories (kcal) per serving. If you are on a low-calorie diet or are watching your intake of sodium, for example, these figures should help you gauge your eating habits and help you balance your meals. Bear in mind, however, that the calculations are fundamentally estimates and are to be followed only in a very general way. The actual quantity of fat, for example, that may be contained in a given portion will vary with the quality of meat you buy or with how much care you take in skimming off cooking fat. If you are on a rigid diet, consult your physician. The analyses are based on the number of portions given as the yield for the recipe, but if the yield reads, "4 to 6 servings," we indicate which number of servings (4, for example) was used.

FOR AUSTRALIAN COOKS

The measurements in this book are given in British Imperial and metric quantities. For best results in Australia, use the metric measures. If using metrics is a problem, adjust the tablespoon quantities for Australia as follows. All other Imperial measures for Great Britain and Australia are the same.

BRITISH	2 tablespoons	3½ tablespoons	4 tablespoons
AUSTRALIAN	2 tablespoons	3 tablespoons	3½ tablespoons

Desirable Weights

Height (without shoes)		Weight (without clothing)		
		Low	Average	High
	Men			
5 feet	3 inches	118	129	141
5	4	122	133	145
5	5	126	137	149
5	6	130	142	155
5	7	134	147	161
5	8	139	151	166
5	9	143	155	170
5	10	147	159	174
5	11	150	163	178
6	—	154	167	183
6	1	158	171	188
6	2	162	175	192
6	3	165	178	195
	Women			
5 feet	— inches	100	109	118
5	1	104	112	121
5	2	107	115	125
5	3	110	118	128
5	4	113	122	132
5	5	116	125	135
5	6	120	129	139
5	7	123	132	142
5	8	126	136	146
5	9	130	140	151
5	10	133	144	156
5	11	137	148	161
6	—	141	152	166

SOURCE: Consumer and Food Economics Institute, Agricultural Research Service, U.S. Department of Agriculture

DESIRABLE WEIGHTS

You can get an idea of what your desirable weight might be by using the table alongside. Locate your height in the left-hand column (without shoes). If you have a small frame, your weight should be no lower than the weight in the "low" column and no higher than that in the "average" column. If you have a large frame, use the "average" and "high" columns to determine your desirable weight range. If your frame is about average, your weight should probably be somewhere near the average for your height.

YIELD

4 servings

Per serving
calories 326, protein 38 g,
fat 15 g, sodium 368 mg,
carbohydrates 5 g,
potassium 828 mg

TIME

20 minutes preparation
20 minutes cooking

INGREDIENTS

1 pound (450 g) fresh salmon fillets
1/2 pound (225 g) scallops
3 egg whites
6 tablespoons (120 ml) evaporated
   skim milk
Salt and freshly ground pepper
Court Bouillon (Recipe 9)
Fresh spinach, washed and trimmed
Lemon wedges
Dill sprigs (optional)

DILL SAUCE

3 ounces (45 g) neufchatel cheese
1/4 cup (60 ml) plain yogurt
1 teaspoon lemon juice
1–2 tablespoons chopped fresh dill or
   1–2 teaspoons dill weed
2 tablespoons minced fresh parsley

Combine the first 3 ingredients in a food processor and add 4 table-spoons (75 ml) of skim milk. Mix until thoroughly blended, adding the remaining milk if mixture is too dry. Chill. Prepare the dill sauce by combining all ingredients thoroughly in a liquidiser or processor. Set aside. Bring court bouillon to a simmering point.

Steam the spinach ① until limp. Drain and reserve on a serving platter. Keep warm.

Using the salmon mixture, shape oval dumplings between 2 serving spoons dipped in cold water ②. Gently drop ovals into the simmering court bouillon and poach for 6 to 8 minutes. Turn and poach for another 6 minutes on the other side ③. As dumplings are finished cooking, place on the bed of steamed spinach and garnish with a little dill sauce, lemon wedges, and dill sprigs. Serve the remaining sauce on the side.

NOTE *You may substitute cod, sole, red snapper, or any other firm whitefish fillets.*

YIELD

4 servings

Per serving
calories 175, protein 12 g,
fat 3 g, sodium 374 mg,
carbohydrates 24 g,
potassium 530 mg

TIME

10 minutes preparation
10 minutes cooking

INGREDIENTS

½ ounce (15 g) butter
1 carrot, peeled and diced
2–3 scallions, thinly sliced
1 tablespoon plain flour
1 tin (13 ounces/365 g) evaporated
  skim milk
6 tablespoons (120 ml) chicken broth
1 package (10 ounces/285 g) frozen
  petite peas, thawed
1–2 tablespoons dry sherry
Minced fresh parsley
Lemon slices

In a 2-quart (2-l) saucepan, melt butter and sauté carrot and scallions ①. Add flour and cook, stirring, until foamy ②. Add the evaporated milk and the broth and bring to a boil, stirring occasionally. Add peas, reduce heat, and simmer until carrots are tender, about 6 to 8 minutes.

Whirl the soup in a blender, a portion at a time, until smooth (or force through a food mill or sieve) ③. Return purée to the pan, stir in the sherry to taste, and heat through. Serve hot or cold, garnished with minced parsley and lemon slices.

NOTE *This is a light soup ideal as an hors d'oeuvre or first course.*

YIELD

4 to 5 servings

Per serving (4)
calories 707, protein 37 g,
fat 40 g, sodium 1028 mg,
carbohydrates 50 g,
potassium 1163 mg

TIME

15 minutes preparation
25 minutes cooking
2 hours chilling

INGREDIENTS

½ pound (225 g) shelled medium shrimp
1 teaspoon olive or safflower oil
2 cloves garlic, minced or crushed
1 small red onion, chopped
1 stalk celery, sliced
1 green pepper, seeded and cut into strips
4 ounces (115 g) brown or long-grain rice
½ pint (300 ml) chicken broth
1 tin (8 ounces/225 g) stewed tomatoes, with juice
Tabasco sauce to taste
1 whole chicken breast, skinned, boned, and slivered

1 chorizo or other spicy sausage, cut into 8 slices
1 avocado
Small red onion, sliced
Green leaf lettuce

DRESSING

4 tablespoons (75 ml) safflower oil
4 tablespoons (75 ml) lemon juice
½ teaspoon dried oregano or thyme leaves
½ teaspoon dry or Dijon-style mustard
¼ teaspoon garlic powder
1 ounce (30 g) minced fresh parsley

Clean the shrimp, removing the veins ①.

In a large stockpot, heat oil and sauté garlic, chopped onion, celery, and green pepper just until softened, about 3 minutes ②. Add rice, broth, tomatoes, Tabasco, chicken, and sausage. Bring to a boil, reduce heat, cover, and simmer 15 minutes. Quickly add shrimp and cook 5 minutes longer, or until rice is tender and shrimp have turned bright pink. Remove from heat and allow to cool slightly.

Combine dressing ingredients in a covered container and shake until creamy. Place salad in serving bowl and add the dressing. Toss lightly. Refrigerate at least 2 hours. When ready to serve, peel, seed, and dice the avocado ③. Garnish with the avocado chunks, red onion slices, and lettuce leaves.

YIELD

4 servings

Per serving

calories 428, protein 58 g, fat 10 g, sodium 567 mg, carbohydrates 17 g, potassium 1057 mg

TIME

10 minutes preparation
15 minutes cooking

INGREDIENTS

1½ pounds (600 g) boneless chicken breasts, skinned

Salt and freshly ground pepper

¼ ounce (7 g) butter

1 teaspoon oil

3 tablespoons finely chopped shallots or scallions

½ pound (225 g) fresh mushrooms, quartered or sliced

2 tablespoons cognac or brandy

1 tin (13 ounces/365 g) evaporated skim milk

2 ounces (60 g) shredded swiss cheese

2 ounces (60 g) crumbled low-fat farmers cheese

1 ounce (30 g) grated parmesan cheese

Minced scallions

Cut each chicken breast into 6 or 7 strips ①. Sprinkle with salt and pepper.

Heat the butter and oil in a heavy skillet and when it is foaming, add the chicken strips. Cook over high heat, stirring and shaking the skillet for 3 to 4 minutes ②. Remove the chicken with a slotted spoon and set aside.

Add the shallots or scallions, mushrooms, and cognac and cook, stirring, for 2 or 3 minutes. Add the evaporated milk and cook down over high heat for about 5 minutes. Stir in the cheeses ③. Add chicken and heat through. Sprinkle parmesan cheese over entire dish and run under the broiler until golden brown. Garnish with scallions and serve hot.

YIELD

4 servings

Per serving
calories 310, protein 23 g,
fat 21 g, sodium 464 mg,
carbohydrates 5 g,
potassium 263 mg

TIME

10 to 15 minutes
  preparation
15 to 20 minutes cooking

INGREDIENTS

6 eggs, separated
2 tablespoons water
¼ teaspoon ground cumin
¼ teaspoon cayenne
¼ pint + 4 tablespoons (240 ml)
  ricotta
3 ounces (90 g) grated monterey jack
  cheese
1 ounce (30 g) grated romano cheese

FILLING

1 ounce (30 g) diced canned green
  chilies, or 2–3 fresh chilies,
  roasted, peeled, and minced
¼ cup (60 ml) Mexican hot sauce
2–3 tablespoons minced cilantro (fresh
  coriander)

Preheat oven to 425° F (215° C—gas mark 7). Prepare the filling by mixing the chilies, hot sauce, and cilantro. Set aside.

With an electric mixer set on high, beat egg whites until they hold a stiff peak ①.

In a separate bowl, beat the egg yolks and add the water, spices, and cheeses. Mix well. Stir one-third of the whites into the yolk mixture ②. Then gently fold in half the remaining whites. Spoon the soufflé mixture into a greased 1-quart (1-l) soufflé dish ③. Add filling and top with remaining soufflé mixture. Set dish into hot oven and bake until puffed and golden, about 15 to 20 minutes. Serve immediately.

YIELD

5 servings

Per serving
calories 106, protein 16 g,
fat 3 g, sodium 147 mg,
carbohydrates 1 g,
potassium 208 mg

TIME

15 minutes preparation
1 hour chilling

INGREDIENTS

1 pound (450 g) peeled small shrimp,
   fresh or frozen
1 tablespoon neufchatel cheese
1 scallion
½–1 teaspoon lemon juice
⅛ teaspoon dill weed

MINCEUR MAYONNAISE

3 egg yolks
1 tablespoon Dijon-style mustard
2 teaspoons white wine vinegar or
   lemon juice
6 tablespoons (120 ml) safflower oil
¼ cup (60 ml) kefir or neufchatel
   cheese
salt and freshly ground pepper

Thaw shrimp if frozen.

Prepare mayonnaise. Place yolks and mustard in liquidiser or food processor ①. Whirl to blend, then slowly add vinegar. When blended, add oil a drop at a time, then increase flow to a slow, steady stream about 1/16 inch (¼ cm) wide ②. Finally mix in kefir or neufchatel cheese and season to taste with salt and pepper. You should have a little over ¼ pint. Measure 1 tablespoon for this recipe, then save remainder for other recipes.

Blend mayonnaise with neufchatel cheese. Mince the scallion ③, then combine with remaining ingredients for salad. Fold in shrimp and chill for 1 hour.

YIELD

4 servings

Per serving
calories 340, protein 21 g,
fat 9 g, sodium 433 mg,
carbohydrates 43 g,
potassium 1251 mg

TIME

10 minutes preparation
15 minutes cooking

INGREDIENTS

1 small red onion, thinly sliced
1½ ounces (45 g) butter
2 tablespoons plain flour
1 ounce (30 g) nonfat dry milk
2 tins (13 ounces/365 g each)
  evaporated skim milk
¼ pint + 4 tablespoons (240 ml)
  skim milk
1 pound (450 g) carrots, peeled and
  thinly sliced
¼–½ teaspoon dried thyme leaves

Sauté onion in butter over medium-high heat until soft ①. Stir in flour and dry milk ② and cook until bubbly. Gradually add evaporated and regular skim milks, stirring well to combine.

Add carrots to soup ③, and bring to boiling point. Reduce heat, and simmer until carrots are tender, about 10 minutes. Add thyme and season to taste. Place soup in liquidiser and purée until smooth. Serve hot.

VARIATIONS For cream of asparagus soup, roughly chop 1 pound (450 g) of fresh asparagus (save some tips for garnish). Add to soup base along with canned milk and simmer until tender, about 8 to 10 minutes. After puréeing, add dry sherry to taste and garnish with sieved hard-cooked egg yolk.

For cream of cauliflower soup, roughly chop 1 medium head of cauliflower. Add to soup base along with milk and simmer 10 minutes. After blending, stir in 2 ounces (60 g) shredded sharp cheddar cheese.

YIELD

4 servings

Per serving
calories 203, protein 22 g,
fat 10 g, sodium 273 mg,
carbohydrates 5 g,
potassium 582 mg

TIME

10 minutes preparation

INGREDIENTS

½ pound (225 g) lean rare roast beef, sliced
1 medium cucumber, peeled in alternate strips
½ pound (225 g) fresh spinach, rinsed and dried
6 tablespoons (120 ml) kefir or neufchatel cheese
1–2 tablespoons freshly grated or prepared horseradish

1 tablespoon skim milk (optional)
1 teaspoon lemon juice
Salt and freshly ground pepper

Cut beef into thin julienne strips. Cut cucumber in half lengthwise ①. Scoop out seeds with spoon ②. Thinly slice ③ and add to roast beef.

Chop spinach and set aside.

Mix remaining ingredients and fold into roast beef mixture. On a serving platter, arrange chopped fresh spinach and add roast beef salad. Chill before serving.

YIELD

4 servings

Per serving
calories 349, protein 32 g,
fat 19 g, sodium 118 mg,
carbohydrates 3 g,
potassium 697 mg

TIME

10 minutes preparation
20 minutes cooking

INGREDIENTS

4 fish steaks or fillets, about 4 to 6
   ounces (150 g) each (sea bass,
   salmon, snapper, or cod)
1 tablespoon cornflour
Minced fresh parsley
chopped pimiento

COURT BOUILLON

¼ pint (150 ml) each water and dry
   white wine
½ small onion, sliced
½ stalk celery, sliced
½ carrot, peeled and sliced
Bouquet garni (1 bay leaf, 1 sprig
   parsley, 1 sprig or pinch thyme,
   6 black peppercorns, tied together
   in a muslin bag)

Combine ingredients for court bouillon in a large saucepan. Bring to a boil, reduce heat, and simmer, covered, for 10 minutes.

Strain court bouillon through a fine sieve or cheesecloth into a large skillet ①. Place fish in hot court bouillon ②, then cover and simmer until fish becomes a creamy, opaque white and flakes easily when tested with a fork ③. The cooking time should be about 7 to 10 minutes, depending upon the thickness of the fish. Carefully remove fish to a heated serving platter.

To make the sauce, scoop up ¼ cup (60 ml) of bouillon and blend in the cornflour until the mixture is smooth. Return bouillon to the pan and cook, stirring until bubbly and thickened. Pour sauce over fish and garnish with parsley and chopped pimiento.

YIELD

4 servings

Per serving
calories 461, protein 49 g,
fat 25 g, sodium 238 mg,
carbohydrates 7 g,
potassium 554 mg

TIME

15 minutes preparation
Overnight marinating
20 minutes cooking

INGREDIENTS

1 chicken, about 3½ pounds (1½ k),
   cut up
¼ pint (150 ml) plain yogurt
2–3 cloves garlic, minced or
   crushed
½ teaspoon each ground cumin and
   ground cinnamon
1 teaspoon each ground turmeric,
   ginger, and coriander
1 ounce (30 g) minced red onion

¼ cup (60 ml) fresh lime juice
Salt and freshly ground pepper
4 lime slices

Prick skin of chicken with a fork ①. Combine remaining ingredients, except lime slices, in a large, shallow bowl and add the chicken. Coat chicken pieces with the mixture ②; cover and refrigerate overnight. Turn once during the marinating ③.

Preheat electric grill or prepare coals for grilling. Place chicken on broiling rack set 3 to 4 inches from the heat. Cook until crisp and cooked on each side, about 8 minutes per side. Serve with lime slices.

NOTE Chicken may be baked in a 375° F (190° C—gas mark 5) oven. Place chicken on lightly greased baking dish, skin side up, and bake for about 45 minutes, or until tender.

YIELD

8 servings

Per serving
calories 428, protein 23 g,
fat 17 g, sodium 1695 mg,
carbohydrates 44 g,
potassium 274 mg

TIME

15 minutes preparation
4 minutes cooking
2 hours chilling

INGREDIENTS

4 quarts (4 l) water
Pinch of salt
1 tablespoon oil
1 pound (450 g) fresh pasta,
    preferably green or orange
½ pound (225 g) cooked small
    shrimp
1 tin (10 ounces/285 g) whole clams,
    drained
1 tin (6 ounces/170 g) crab meat
1 red or green pepper, thinly sliced

1 small cucumber, peeled in alternate
    strips, then quartered and thinly
    sliced
1 ounce (30 g) each capers, minced
    fresh parsley, and sliced ripe olives
6 tablespoons (120 ml) kefir cheese
6 tablespoons (120 ml) low-calorie
    Vinaigrette (Recipe 16)
Green leaf lettuce

Bring water, salt, and oil to a boil in a large kettle. Add pasta and cook about 4 minutes, or until *al dente*. Rinse, drain ①, and place in large bowl.

Add the remaining ingredients except the cheese and the dressing. Mix gently. Whisk the cheese and vinaigrette together to form a creamy sauce ②, then pour onto salad, toss gently ③, and chill for a couple of hours.

To serve, place salad in a large bowl and surround with green leaf lettuce.

YIELD

4 servings

Per serving
calories 522, protein 40 g,
fat 28 g, sodium 2218 mg,
carbohydrates 24 g,
potassium 1185 mg

TIME

15 minutes preparation
30 minutes marinating
15 minutes cooking

INGREDIENTS

4 chicken legs (thigh and drumstick),
  boned
6 tablespoons (120 ml) oyster sauce
2–3 cloves garlic, crushed
1 tablespoon grated green root ginger
1 each green and red bell pepper
1 courgette
1 yellow crookneck squash
1 tablespoon sesame or safflower oil
1 red or yellow onion, sliced

8 flowerets each broccoli and
  cauliflower
¼ cup (60 ml) sherry or chicken or
  beef broth
1–2 teaspoons sambel oelek
  (Indonesian chile paste)
2 ounces (60 g) walnut halves
2 tablespoons tamari or regular soy
  sauce
Cooked brown or white rice

Marinate the chicken legs for 30 minutes in a mixture of oyster sauce, garlic, and ginger ①.

Slice peppers and squashes into julienne strips and set aside.

Over medium-high heat, heat the sesame oil in a wok or large pan until almost smoking. Add the chicken and onion slices and toss ②, cooking for 3 to 4 minutes. Add the remaining ingredients ③. Stir to mix well and cook until vegetables are tender-crisp. Serve over brown or white rice.

YIELD

4 servings

Per serving
calories 264, protein 30 g,
fat 10 g, sodium 1009 mg,
carbohydrates 5 g,
potassium 785 mg

TIME

5 minutes preparation
2 hours marinating
12 minutes cooking

INGREDIENTS

4 swordfish steaks, about 6 ounces
  (170 g) each
2 teaspoons safflower oil
2 tablespoons tamari or regular soy
  sauce
1 tablespoon lemon juice
6 tablespoons (120 ml) dry white
  wine
1 teaspoon chopped fresh tarragon or
  ¼ teaspoon dried
1 ounce (30 g) minced scallions,
  white parts only

2 tablespoons Dijon-style mustard
2 tablespoons evaporated skim milk,
  kefir, or neufchatel cheese
Lemon wedges or slices

Place steaks in a shallow baking dish. Combine oil, soy sauce, lemon juice, wine, tarragon, and scallions, then pour over fish ①. Turn steaks to coat other side, cover, and refrigerate for 2 hours.

Blend together the mustard and milk or cheese ②. Preheat the grill.

Grill steaks 3 to 4 inches from the heat for about 12 minutes or until fish browns lightly. During last few minutes, divide mustard mixture among the steaks ③, spreading a little on each. Serve with lemon wedges or slices.

ROAST CHICKEN WITH LEMON-DILL SAUCE

YIELD

4 servings

Per serving
calories 475, protein 48 g,
fat 25 g, sodium 438 mg,
carbohydrates 6 g,
potassium 554 mg

TIME

10 minutes preparation
1½ hours cooking

INGREDIENTS

1 roasting chicken, about 3½ pounds
   (1½ k)
5 sprigs fresh dill or 1½ teaspoons dill
   weed
1 red onion, quartered
1 lemon, quartered
⅓ ounce (10 g) butter
6 tablespoons (120 ml) dry white
   wine

¼ pint (150 ml) chicken broth
1 teaspoon cornflour
Additional dill sprigs and lemon
   wedges to garnish

Preheat oven to 350° F (180° C—gas mark 4).

Place chicken on roasting rack and put 4 sprigs (or 1 teaspoon dill weed) and quartered onion inside bird ①. Rub surface of chicken with lemon and spread with butter ②. Place 2 wedges of lemon inside, then place chicken in roasting pan and add wine and broth to pan. Roast for 1½ hours or until tender, basting with liquid every 15 to 20 minutes.

Transfer chicken from pan to a warmed platter and keep warm. Chop the remaining sprig of dill.

Strain the pan juices into a saucepan ③. Reserve 2 tablespoons of liquid and mix with the cornflour until smooth. Pour cornflour mixture into juices and bring to a boil. Whisk until smooth, add remaining dill and lemon, and then check for seasoning. Carve chicken and serve with sauce. Garnish with extra dill and lemon if desired.

YIELD

4 to 6 servings

Per serving
calories 163, protein 12 g,
fat 10 g, sodium 258 mg,
carbohydrates 6 g,
potassium 563 mg

TIME

20 minutes preparation
10 to 12 minutes cooking

INGREDIENTS

1 package (10 ounces/285 g) frozen
   chopped spinach, cooked and well
   drained
2 egg yolks
Freshly ground pepper
Ground nutmeg
4 egg whites
1½ ounces (45 g) freshly grated
   romano or parmesan cheese

FILLING

½ pound (225 g) fresh mushrooms,
   sliced or chopped
¼ ounce (7 g) butter
6 tablespoons (120 ml) kefir cheese
   or neufchatel cheese

Preheat oven to 375° F (190° C—gas mark 5).

Mix cooked spinach with egg yolks. Season to taste with pepper and nutmeg.

Beat the egg whites until they form soft peaks. Stir one-third of the egg whites into the spinach mixture, then fold in remaining whites.

Line a baking sheet with buttered parchment paper or foil. Spread the spinach mixture on the paper or foil to a rectangle about 8 by 12 inches (20 by 30 cm) ①. Sprinkle with cheese and bake for 10 to 12 minutes.

Meanwhile, sauté mushrooms for filling in butter until just softened. Mix with cheese and set aside.

Turn out roulade onto a clean cloth or length of foil. Spread filling evenly over spinach, leaving ½ inch (1½ cm) around the edge ② (so filling won't ooze out when rolled). Roll up ③. Slice and serve warm.

CRAB MEAT AND ARTICHOKE SALAD

YIELD

4 servings

Per serving
calories 110, protein 8 g,
fat 6 g, sodium 658 mg,
carbohydrates 3 g,
potassium 185 mg

TIME

5 minutes preparation
2 hours chilling

INGREDIENTS

1 tin (10 ounces/285 g) artichoke
   hearts
1 tin (6 ounces/170 g) crab meat
1 tin (2 ounces/60 g) sliced ripe olives
1 teaspoon grated lemon rind

LOW-CALORIE VINAIGRETTE

6 tablespoons (120 ml) chicken broth
3 tablespoons vegetable oil
¼ cup (60 ml) plus 1 tablespoon red
   wine vinegar or lemon juice
1 teaspoon dry or Dijon-style mustard
Salt and freshly ground pepper

Combine ingredients for dressing in a small bowl and blend with a wire whisk ①. This will make between ¼ and ½ pint of vinaigrette. For this recipe you'll need ¼ cup (60 ml); save the remainder for another use.

Drain the artichokes and crab meat ②. Combine artichokes, crab meat, olives, and lemon rind, then stir in ¼ cup (60 ml) vinaigrette ③. Chill for 2 or more hours.

NOTE If desired, add fresh minced parsley, chopped hard-cooked egg, or ½ teaspoon dried herb of your choice.

YIELD

4 servings

Per serving
calories 271, protein 8 g,
fat 2 g, sodium 483 mg,
carbohydrates 50 g,
potassium 419 mg

TIME

10 minutes preparation
25 minutes cooking

INGREDIENTS

2 red onions
2–3 courgettes
1 green pepper
1 tablespoon olive oil
3 cloves garlic, minced or crushed
1 tin (16 ounces/450 g) whole
   tomatoes, drained
6 tablespoons (120 ml) dry red wine
1–2 teaspoons chopped fresh basil
Salt
Freshly ground pepper
1 pound (450 g) cooked pasta

Chop onions finely ①. Halve and then thinly slice the courgettes ②. Seed and core, then slice the green pepper ③.

Heat oil in large saucepan and sauté first onions, then courgettes and garlic until softened. Crush tomatoes and add, cooking briefly. Add remaining ingredients and simmer 15 minutes. Serve sauce over hot, drained pasta.

NOTE This sauce also works well as an accompaniment to lamb or pork chops, or as a filling for an omelet.

YIELD

4 servings

Per serving
calories 365, protein 55 g,
fat 11 g, sodium 276 mg,
carbohydrates 6 g,
potassium 555 mg

TIME

10 minutes preparation
20 minutes cooking

INGREDIENTS

8 boneless chicken breasts, about
  2 pounds (900 g)
1 ounce (30 g) plain flour
1 ounce (30 g) grated parmesan
  cheese
½ ounce (15 g) butter
1 tablespoon safflower oil
8 thin slices prosciutto
8 thin slices provolone cheese

Pound chicken to a thickness of ¼ inch (¾ cm) ①. Stir together the flour and cheese, then coat chicken in flour-cheese mixture ②.

Heat butter and oil in a wide frying pan and sauté half the chicken until golden (3 to 4 minutes per side) ③. Do not crowd pan or chicken will color unevenly. Keep cooked chicken warm while sautéeing remaining pieces.

Preheat grill. Top each chicken piece with 1 slice of prosciutto and 1 slice of cheese. Broil until cheese is golden and bubbly. Serve hot.

FRUITED TOFU-SHRIMP SAUTÉ

YIELD

4 servings

Per serving
calories 198, protein 23 g,
fat 7 g, sodium 130 mg,
carbohydrates 11 g,
potassium 327 mg

TIME

5 minutes preparation
6 minutes cooking

INGREDIENTS

¼ ounce (7 g) butter
1 teaspoon safflower oil
2 cloves garlic, minced or crushed
⅔ pound (200 g) shelled medium
   shrimp, cleaned and deveined
1 pound (450 g) tofu, cut in 1-inch
   (2½-cm) cubes
2 ounces (60 g) each red and green
   seedless grapes
¼ cup (60 ml) lemon juice
1 ounce (30 g) minced fresh parsley
4 lemon wheels for garnish

In a large nonstick skillet, heat butter and oil over medium heat. Add garlic, shrimp, and tofu; sauté until shrimp just begin to turn pink, about 4 minutes ①.

Push food in skillet to edges of pan and warm grapes briefly in center ②. All at once, add lemon juice and parsley. Swirl pan to distribute juices and gently mix fruit with seafood.

Transfer mixture to a warmed serving platter or individual dishes and garnish with lemon wheels if desired ③.

LAMB AND VEGETABLE CURRY

YIELD

4 servings

*Per serving
(without garnishes)*
calories 293, protein 28 g,
fat 14 g, sodium 352 mg,
carbohydrates 13 g,
potassium 1018 mg

TIME

15 minutes preparation
30 minutes cooking

INGREDIENTS

I pound (450 g) lean boneless lamb
½ ounce (15 g) butter
I teaspoon safflower oil
2–3 cloves garlic, minced or crushed
I onion, chopped
½ teaspoon each ground cardamom,
   coriander, and turmeric
¼ teaspoon ground cinnamon
¼ teaspoon minced green root ginger
I–3 teaspoons curry powder, depending on
   taste
¼ pint + 4 tablespoons (240 ml) plain
   yogurt
¼ pint + 4 tablespoons (240 ml) chicken
   broth
I stalk celery, sliced
½ pound (225 g) fresh mushrooms, sliced
½ pound (225 g) asparagus or broccoli,
   cut in 1-inch (2½-cm) lengths
Cooked bulgur or rice
I½ ounces (45 g) shredded raw carrots

GARNISHES

Unsalted raw cashews
Raisins
Plain yogurt
Sliced scallions
Lime wedges

Cut lamb into 1-inch (2½-cm) cubes ①. Set aside.

Heat butter and oil in a large skillet, and sauté garlic and onion for 3 minutes, stirring often. Add lamb and brown cubes on all sides ②.

Add spices, yogurt, broth, celery, and mushrooms to skillet and simmer, covered, for 15 minutes. Add asparagus or broccoli on top of mixture in skillet and steam for an additional 10 minutes ③.

Place curry on a bed of bulgur or rice. Garnish with shredded carrots and serve with condiments, if desired.

GINGERED CHICKEN THIGHS

YIELD

4 servings

Per serving
calories 353, protein 31 g,
fat 22 g, sodium 508 mg,
carbohydrates 3 g,
potassium 323 mg

TIME

10 minutes preparation
25 minutes cooking

INGREDIENTS

1 tablespoon safflower oil
2 cloves garlic, minced or crushed
8 chicken thighs
1 tablespoon lemon juice
1 tablespoon grated green root ginger
2 teaspoons arrowroot or cornflour
1 tablespoon soy sauce
Salt and freshly ground pepper

Preheat oven to 450° F (230° C—gas mark 8). In a heatproof and ovenproof casserole or skillet heat oil over medium-high heat. Sauté garlic briefly, then add chicken, skin side down, and sauté until golden brown, about 5 minutes ①.

Turn the chicken and distribute the lemon juice and ginger evenly over the chicken ②. Cover and bake in oven for 15 to 20 minutes.

Remove chicken from oven and place on a serving platter. Thicken the pan juices with a mixture of arrowroot and soy sauce ③. Season to taste and serve.

YIELD

4 servings

Per serving
calories 296, protein 31 g,
fat 12 g, sodium 463 mg,
carbohydrates 14 g,
potassium 983 mg

TIME

10 minutes preparation
Overnight marinating
8 minutes cooking

INGREDIENTS

1 pound (450 g) flank steak, thinly
   sliced
1 tablespoon soy sauce
2 cloves garlic, minced
1 tablespoon grated green root ginger
1/4 cup (60 ml) dry white wine or
   vermouth
1 tablespoon cornflour
1 tablespoon safflower oil
1 bunch broccoli, flowerets and stems
   cut diagonally in bite-sized pieces

1 small red onion, sliced
1/4 pint (150 ml) plain yogurt
Minced scallions or fresh parsley

Marinate the steak overnight in a mixture of soy sauce, garlic, ginger, 2 tablespoons of the wine, and the cornflour ①. Remove garlic and ginger, and discard. Reserve marinade.

Add half the oil to a very hot wok or frying pan, and stir-fry the broccoli and onion, stirring constantly until the broccoli turns bright green, about 2 minutes ②. Add the remaining wine, cover, and cook over high heat for 1 to 2 minutes. Turn onto a platter and arrange the flowerets pointing outward.

Heat the remaining oil and cook the beef slices, stirring constantly for 1 to 2 minutes, until brown. Add marinade mixture and stir in yogurt ③, then pour out onto center of broccoli. Garnish with minced scallions or parsley.

YIELD

4 servings

Per serving

calories 135, protein 6 g, fat 4 g, sodium 510 mg, carbohydrates 18 g, potassium 523 mg

TIME

10 minutes preparation
40 minutes cooking

INGREDIENTS

1 small spaghetti squash
¾ pint (425 ml) chicken or vegetable
   broth
1 pound (450 g) baby carrots, peeled
1 tablespoon vermouth or dry white
   wine
1 teaspoon curry powder
1 teaspoon lemon juice
1 teaspoon minced fresh parsley
3–4 tablespoons kefir or neufchatel
   cheese

Cut the squash in half and place face down on a steamer (if halves won't fit into your steamer, cut in quarters). Steam squash until tender, about 30 minutes, then using a fork, pull strands from the squash to have "spaghetti" ①. Keep warm on a shallow serving bowl or platter.

Bring the broth to a boil. Add the carrots and cook, covered, for 8 minutes or until just tender-crisp. Drain and reserve stock.

Combine 2 or 3 tablespoons of the stock with the vermouth, curry, lemon juice, parsley, and cheese. Add carrots ② and toss gently ③. Serve atop the squash and then garnish with additional minced parsley if desired.

JAMAICAN LAMB CHOPS

YIELD

4 servings

Per serving
calories 229, protein 22 g,
fat 5 g, sodium 186 mg,
carbohydrates 17 g,
potassium 597 mg

TIME

10 minutes preparation
30 minutes cooking

INGREDIENTS

4 loin lamb chops, each ¾ inch
  (2 cm) thick, trimmed
3 ounces (90 g) sliced red onions
¼ pint (150 ml) beef broth
4 tablespoons (75 ml) port or madeira
  wine
3 ounces (90 g) dried apricots or
  peaches
1 tablespoon grated green root ginger
  or ½ teaspoon ground ginger

2 teaspoons instant coffee powder
Salt and pepper
1 teaspoon cornflour (optional)
Lemon or lime slices

In a large skillet, brown the meat with the onions ①. If meat is very lean, you may have to add a little oil.

Meanwhile, in a saucepan, heat the broth and wine and then add the dried fruit, ginger, and coffee ②, stirring to dissolve the instant coffee. Pour the liquid over the meat ③ and simmer, covered, for 15 to 20 minutes. Turn frequently to mix ingredients well.

Taste sauce and season to taste with salt and pepper. Thicken cooking liquid with cornflour if desired, and garnish with lemon or lime slices.

YIELD

2 servings

Per serving (omelet only)
calories 195, protein 13 g,
fat 12 g, sodium 132 mg,
carbohydrates 2 g,
potassium 168 mg

TIME

8 minutes preparation
8 minutes cooking

INGREDIENTS

¼ cup (60 ml) skim milk
4 eggs, separated
1 tablespoon brandy
¼ ounce (7 g) butter
Savory Shrimp Salad (Recipe 6)

Beat together the milk, egg yolks, and brandy ①. Beat egg whites until they are stiff but not dry ②, then stir one-third of the whites into the yolk mixture. Gently fold in the remainder of the whites ③.

Preheat the grill. Over medium-high heat, melt the butter in an oven-proof 9-inch (23-cm) skillet. Add the batter and cover. As the omelet cooks, slash it with a knife to the bottom of the crust to permit the heat to penetrate and cook the eggs. After 5 minutes, remove cover and transfer to the grill to set the mixture. Grill until the omelet is a golden color, about 3 minutes.

Remove omelet from the skillet and pile on shrimp salad. Garnish with a sprig of dill or watercress.

YIELD

4 servings

Per serving
calories 87, protein 2 g,
fat 2 g, sodium 119 mg,
carbohydrates 9 g,
potassium 338 mg

TIME

20 minutes preparation
25 minutes cooking

INGREDIENTS

6–8 broccoli flowerets
2 carrots, peeled and diced
1/4 pound (115 g) fresh green beans,
    trimmed and cut in small diagonal
    slices
1/4 ounce (7 g) butter
2 tablespoons finely chopped shallots
1/2 red or green pepper, cut in julienne
    strips (optional)
1/4 pint (150 ml) dry white wine
Salt and freshly ground pepper
4 large iceburg lettuce leaves

Cook broccoli, carrots, and beans in simmering water for 8 to 10 minutes. Drain.

In a large skillet, melt butter and sauté shallots and peppers until softened. Add half the wine and cook over high heat for 1 minute. Mix in vegetables and season to taste with salt and pepper.

Preheat oven to 400° F (200° C—gas mark 6). Bring 1 quart (1 l) of water to a boil. Add the lettuce leaves and simmer for 3 to 4 minutes. Remove lettuce carefully, and spread out each leaf on paper toweling ①. Trim away a 1-inch (2½-cm)-thick center rib from each leaf ②. Spoon the vegetable mixture evenly onto the center of each leaf. Bring sides of lettuce up over filling ③.

Lightly grease a shallow baking dish. Place the leaves, folded side down, in dish and pour in remaining wine. Cover dish with a lid or foil and bake for 10 minutes. Serve hot.

YIELD

4 servings

Per serving
calories 238, protein 8 g,
fat 8 g, sodium 183 mg,
carbohydrates 35 g,
potassium 1203 mg

TIME

10 minutes preparation
2 hours chilling

INGREDIENTS

1 pawpaw
2 medium cantaloupes
6 tablespoons (120 ml) plain yogurt
6 tablespoons (120 ml) kefir cheese
1/4 pint + 4 tablespoons (240 ml)
    skim or evaporated skim milk
1/4 teaspoon each ground cinnamon
    and nutmeg
Mint sprigs

Peel ① and seed ② the pawpaw. Cut the cantaloupes in half and remove seeds. Scoop out almost all of the flesh. Flute edges ③.

Place yogurt, cheese, skim milk, spices, and flesh of cantaloupes into a liquidiser or food processor. Blend until smooth and creamy, then chill. Fill melon halves with soup and garnish with mint.

GINGER-FROSTED FRUIT

YIELD

4 servings

Per serving
calories 212, protein 3 g,
fat 2 g, sodium 37 mg,
carbohydrates 48 g,
potassium 854 mg

TIME

15 minutes preparation
2 hours chilling

INGREDIENTS

¼ pint + 4 tablespoons (240 ml)
    plain yogurt
1 ounce (30 g) chopped crystallized
    ginger
2–3 tablespoons honey
1 teaspoon lemon juice
1 pound (450 g) sliced mixed fresh
    fruits (strawberries, bananas,
    oranges, and so on)
4 sprigs mint

In a bowl, combine yogurt, ginger, honey, and lemon juice; mix thoroughly ①.

Pour mixture over fruits ② and cover. Refrigerate for at least 2 hours to marry flavors.

To serve, spoon fruits into small dessert dishes or parfait glasses. Garnish with a sprig of mint.

COLD CUCUMBER AND MINT SOUP

YIELD

4 servings

Per serving
calories 191, protein 8 g,
fat 15 g, sodium 254 mg,
carbohydrates 7 g,
potassium 283 mg

TIME

10 minutes preparation
2 hours chilling

INGREDIENTS

1/4 pint (150 ml) each plain yogurt
   and kefir cheese
2 cucumbers, peeled and coarsely
   chopped
1 teaspoon lemon juice
1 tablespoon chopped fresh mint
1/4 pint (150 ml) cold club soda
Salt
Freshly ground white pepper

Place yogurt and kefir in food processor. Briefly whirl to blend, then place cucumber and remaining ingredients in processor and process off and on until cucumber is finely diced. Season to taste with salt and pepper.

CEVICHE

YIELD

4 servings

Per serving
calories 123, protein 19 g,
fat 3 g, sodium 254 mg,
carbohydrates 4 g,
potassium 437 mg

TIME

10 minutes preparation
Overnight marinating

INGREDIENTS

1 pound (450 g) combination of
   scallops, small shrimp, squid, and
   white fish fillets
2 scallions, minced
6–8 cherry tomatoes, halved
3 tablespoons lime juice
2 teaspoons oil
1 tablespoon chopped fresh cilantro
   (coriander) or parsley
1/4 teaspoon oregano leaves

Tabasco
Salt and pepper
Avocado slices

Combine seafood, scallions, cherry tomatoes, lime juice, oil, herbs, Tabasco, and salt and pepper to taste. Cover and refrigerate overnight. When ready to serve, place in serving bowl and garnish with avocado slices.

CITRUS FRUIT SALAD

YIELD

6 servings

Per serving
calories 98, protein 2 g,
fat 2 g, sodium 95 mg,
carbohydrates 18 g,
potassium 535 mg

TIME

10 minutes preparation

INGREDIENTS

1 bunch watercress, washed, dried,
 and stems twisted off
1 bunch escarole, washed and dried
2 each oranges and grapefruit, peeled
 and segmented
4 tablespoons (75 ml) orange juice

¼ cup (60 ml) lemon juice
1 tablespoon safflower oil
¼ teaspoon dry mustard
Salt and freshly ground pepper

Break watercress and escarole into bite-sized pieces. Place in salad bowl, along with orange and grapefruit sections.

In a small bowl, mix together the orange juice, lemon juice, oil, mustard, and salt and pepper to taste. Pour over salad and toss gently.

COLIN'S COTTAGE-CHEESE MUFFINS

YIELD

8 to 12 muffins

Per serving
calories 240, protein 17 g,
fat 8 g, sodium 792 mg,
carbohydrates 24 g,
potassium 293 mg

TIME

10 minutes preparation
30 minutes baking

INGREDIENTS

3 eggs, lightly beaten
1 large onion, finely chopped
2 tablespoons soy sauce
1 tablespoon safflower oil
2–3 tablespoons nonfat dry milk
1 tablespoon wheat germ
8 ounces (225 g) low-fat curd cheese
8 ounces (225 g) rolled oats
2 tablespoons minced fresh parsley

1 teaspoon ground sage
2 teaspoons Vegemite or tahini
 (optional)

Preheat oven to 375° F (190° C—gas mark 5). Lightly oil a muffin tin.

Combine all ingredients in a bowl and stir well. Pour mixture into muffin cups and bake for 30 minutes. Serve warm.

INDEX

The following numbers refer to recipe numbers, not page numbers.

Artichoke and Crab Meat Salad, **16**

Beef: and Broccoli in Yogurt Sauce, **22**; Roast Beef and Cucumbers, **8**

Cantaloupe-Pawpaw Soup, **27**
Carrots: Curried, with Spaghetti Squash, **23**; Soup, Cream of, **7**
Ceviche, Seafood, **30**
Chicken: Roast, with Lemon-Dill Sauce, **14**; Saltimbocca, **18**; Tandoori, Grilled, **10**; Thighs, Gingered, **21**; Villeroi, **4**; and Walnut Stir-Fry, Spicy, **12**
Court Bouillon, **9**
Crab Meat and Artichoke Salad, **16**
Cucumber and Mint Soup, Cold, **29**

Egg Dishes: Soufflé Olé, **5**; Soufflé Omelet with Shrimp Salad, **25**

Fish: Poached, **9**; Salmon Quenelles, **1**; Swordfish Steaks, Marinated, **13**
Fruit: Citrus Salad, **31**; Ginger-Frosted, **28**
Fruited Tofu-Shrimp Sauté, **19**

Lamb: Chops, Jamaican, **24**; and Vegetable Curry, **20**

Muffins, Colin's Cottage Cheese, **32**

Pasta with Provençal Sauce, **17**
Pawpaw-Cantaloupe Soup, **27**
Pea Soup (Potage Saint-Germain), **2**

Salads: California Seafood, **11**; Chilled Paella, **3**; Citrus Fruit, **31**; Crab Meat and Artichoke, **16**; Savory Shrimp, **6, 25**
Salmon Quenelles, **1**

Sauces: Dill, **1**; Low-Calorie Vinaigrette, **16**; Minceur Mayonnaise, **6**
Seafood: California Seafood Salad, **11**; Ceviche, **30**; Chilled Paella Salad, **3**; Crab Meat and Artichoke Salad, **16**; Fruited Tofu-Shrimp Sauté, **19**; Savory Shrimp Salad, **6, 25**
Soufflé Olé, **5**
Soufflé Omelet, **25**
Soups: Cold Cucumber and Mint, **29**; Cream of Carrot, **7**; Pawpaw-Cantaloupe, **27**; Potage Saint-Germain, **2**
Spaghetti Squash with Curried Carrots, **23**
Spinach Roulade with Mushroom Filling, **15**
Swordfish Steaks, Marinated, **13**

Vegetable and Lamb Curry, **20**
Vegetables Baked in Lettuce, **26**